Uncle Jacques
56 years old

Mrs. Durand
39 years old

Mr. Durand
42 years old

Gran Bourrel
68 years old

Grandpa Durand
79 years old

Philippe
8 years old

Michèle
10 years old

Jean Pierre
13 years old

A NEW COMMUNITY... IN EUROPE

by
Brian Haigh

Macdonald Educational

What is this book about?

Twelve countries now belong to the European Community. It is one of the richest and most densely-populated areas in the world. This book will help you to understand how and why the Community came about. It will also show you how the Community is trying to help its members.

How to use this book

Part of this book is a story. But, all through, you'll see sections like this one which look as if they've been torn from a reporter's notebook. They are marked 'Evidence'. All the pictures in these sections are of real people and how they lived. They tell the real story of how a new community has been formed in Western Europe after World War Two. See if you can decide whether or not it is a good thing to be a part of this community.

Factual Adviser
Professor Stephen Holt
Professor of European Studies
University of Kent, at Canterbury

Educational Adviser
Alistair Ross
Principal Lecturer in Primary Education
Polytechnic of North London

Series Editor Nicole Lagneau

Book Editor Stephen White-Thomson

Teacher Panel
Tim Firth, Rita Ward, Judith Lockley

Design Sally Boothroyd

Production Rosemary Bishop

Picture Research Kathy Lockley

A MACDONALD BOOK

© Macdonald & Company (Publishers) Ltd 1985

First published in Great Britain in 1985 by Macdonald & Company (Publishers) Ltd
London & Sydney
A BPCC plc company

Printed and bound in Great Britain by Purnell & Sons (Book Production) Ltd, Paulton, nr. Bristol

Macdonald & Company (Publishers) Ltd
Maxwell House
74 Worship Street
London EC2A 2EN

British Library Cataloguing in Publication Data
Haigh, B.
   A new community – in Europe.——(People then and now)
   1. European communities——History
   I. Title   II. Series
   341.24′22′09   HC241.2
   ISBN 0–356–11226–8

Contents

Michèle meets Anna

Michèle looked impatiently around the room in the town hall. 'Mum, I wonder which of the girls is Anna?' 'Ssh, Michèle!' said her Mum. 'Listen to what the mayor is saying.' Michèle sighed. 'The mayor has said enough already. I'm sure the German visitors can't understand a word.'

'We are very proud of our town of Falaise,' said the mayor. 'In 1945, at the end of World War Two, the town lay in ruins. But since then we have rebuilt not only our homes and factories, but also the friendships which the war ended. Now the people of Europe are working more closely together for peace and prosperity.'

'Mum, is that Anna over there?' Michèle whispered, pointing to a girl who was listening carefully to what the mayor was saying. Mrs. Durand pretended not to hear. The mayor carried on speaking. 'Exchange visits between schools are very important. Young people, like you, get the chance to learn another language, and make new friends. I hope that your stay will be enjoyable and that you will make many visits to our town.' Michèle joined in the polite applause, and then bounded off to find Anna. Anna was standing in a corner, looking nervously around the room.

'Hello. Are you Anna?' 'Yes. And you are Michèle?' 'Yes. Come and meet my parents. Mum, Dad. Meet Anna Rack . . . Rok . . .' 'Rockwitz,' said Anna helpfully. Michèle tried again. 'Rockwids . . . Rockvit . . .' 'Almost. That's better,' laughed Anna. 'It's very nice to meet you,' said Mr. Durand.

The tower of St. Gervase church stands out above the roofs of Falaise. This peaceful view of Falaise was taken a few years before World War Two began.

Where has our house gone? Falaise was badly bombed when it was caught between the British and American allies and the retreating Germans in August 1944.

This is what the centre of Falaise looks like today. As you can see, it has been carefully rebuilt, like many other towns in this part of France.

'How was your trip from Germany?' 'It was quite long, but I enjoyed it.' 'Anna, you must be very tired. Michèle, why don't you and Anna thank the mayor, and then we can go home and see what your brothers have been up to,' said Mrs. Durand.

A few minutes later, they all set off on the short walk home. The two girls chatted happily together as if they had known each other for ages. 'How many brothers do you have?' asked Anna. 'Two. Jean Pierre is thirteen and Philippe is my baby brother! He's eight. I'm the one in the middle.' 'You are ten, aren't you? The same age as me.' 'That's right. Look, here's our house. There's Philippe and Jean Pierre waving at us from the window.'

A day out with Gran

'Hurry up, girls,' Mrs. Durand called up the stairs. 'Gran Bourrel is waiting to take you to the castle. If you don't leave soon, you'll miss the tour.' 'Won't be a minute,' shouted Michèle. Soon, Michèle and Anna came running down the stairs. They grabbed their anoraks and chased after Gran who had gone on ahead. They caught up with her just before she reached the castle.

'Oh, there you are!' said Gran. 'The tour is about to start. Here are the tickets. One for you, Anna. And one for Michèle.' Inside the castle, the guide started to tell them about William the Conqueror who was born there many centuries ago. But the girls were not listening. They couldn't wait to climb the tower.

'Be careful of the steps. They are very worn,' said the guide as he led them into the tower. 'Look how thick the walls are. And look at these funny little windows,' said Michèle, trying to peer through them. 'No wonder it's so dark in here. It must be really spooky at night-time!' At last they reached the top. 'Come along, Gran. Look at the view! There's St. Gervase church.' 'It's certainly worth the effort,' puffed Gran.

When they reached the bottom of the steps, they thanked the guide and then walked with Gran through the castle gardens. Gran put her arms around Anna and Michèle's shoulders. 'You ought to visit me in Caen. But I expect you're too busy.' 'Is Caen your home?' asked Anna. 'Yes. I've lived there all my life, even during the war.' 'But I thought Caen was destroyed in the war,' said Michèle.

Gran sat down on a bench, and sighed. 'Yes, Caen was heavily bombed. We were very frightened. It was a terrible time. We had to beg for food and sleep in barns. We were separated from our friends and families. Finally, in 1944, the allies came to free us from the German soldiers who were occupying our city. I don't want anything like it to happen ever again. We don't want any more wars. It's up to young people like you to make sure that the people of Europe are friends so that we can all live in peace.'

'Well, we're good friends,' said Michèle, looking across at Anna, who nodded. 'Yes, and that's a start,' agreed Gran. 'Come on, you two. We must be getting home.'

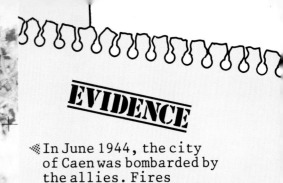

In June 1944, the city of Caen was bombarded by the allies. Fires blazed for 11 days. The battle for Caen raged for over two months.

Normandy
Caen
Falaise
Paris

FRANCE

The Germans occupied France in 1940. In 1944 the allies landed in Normandy and fought to push the German armies back towards Paris.

Refugees from the French town of Caen. Young and old alike were forced to leave their homes as the allies fought a vicious battle to drive the Germans out of Caen.

11

A museum visit

Anna and Michèle walked quietly across the museum floor and stood gazing at the tapestry. 'But it can't be 900 years old. The colours look so bright,' whispered Anna. 'Well that's what it says on the tape,' said Michèle. 'I'll rewind it and we can listen again.'

'The Bayeux Tapestry tells the story of the conquest of England by Duke William of Normandy. It is over 70 metres long and 50 centimetres high. A group of English ladies made it for Odo, bishop of Bayeux in the eleventh century . . .' 'There, I told you,' said Michèle. 'That makes it even older than Gran!' 'Is Duke William of Normandy the same person as William the Conqueror who was born in Falaise castle?' asked Anna. 'Yes, I think so,' said Michèle, and turned back to admire the tapestry.

Across the room, Jean Pierre was firing questions at the guide. 'Why did Duke William want to conquer England?' he asked. The guide laughed. 'If you've got all day to spare maybe I can start to tell you! I'll try to explain in a few words. Duke William believed that he had a right to the English throne and as king of England he would be wealthier and stronger.' 'So William wanted to be more powerful?' asked Jean Pierre. 'Yes. He was just like many of the other great, and not so great, figures of history.'

'Who do you mean?' asked Jean Pierre. The guide scratched his head. 'Where can I begin? There was the Roman emperor, Julius Caesar; the French emperor, Napoleon; and, of course, Hitler.'

12

'The plum pudding in danger!' Greedy for power, Napoleon (1769–1821) carves for himself a large slice of Europe. Napoleon was the emperor of France. He ruled a large part of Europe for a short time. His empire came to an end with his defeat at the battle of Waterloo in 1815.

EVIDENCE

The face of the Roman emperor Julius Caesar (100–44 BC) was well known throughout Europe. Roman rule over much of Europe lasted for several centuries.

Crowds welcomed Adolf Hitler into Czechoslovakia in 1939. Hitler dreamed of uniting most German-speaking peoples. During his time in power he brought disaster to Europe.

Jean Pierre interrupted. 'Our history teacher has told us all about Napoleon. At least he wasn't all bad, like Hitler. Napoleon once controlled almost the whole of Europe except a little corner in the south-west, isn't that right?'

The guide folded his arms, and nodded. 'Yes, but Napoleon's empire didn't last for very long.' 'Neither did Hitler's control of Europe,' added Jean Pierre. 'Luckily not,' the guide went on. 'Where would we be now if he had been successful? People who have been greedy for power have done some terrible things.'

'I hope the last war has taught us all a lesson,' the guide said in a serious voice. 'How do you mean?' asked Jean Pierre. 'Well, that it's better to settle our differences by talking, not fighting, about them. The European Community has shown how countries that were once enemies can now work together in a friendly way. The Community wants to prevent someone like Hitler ever getting his own way again.' Jean Pierre was about to ask how it could do this when Michèle called, 'Come on, Jean Pierre, it's time to go.' The guide shrugged his shoulders. 'You'd better go.' Jean Pierre thanked him and walked outside to join Anna and Michèle.

Hitler's Europe

Life in Germany was very hard after its defeat in World War One (1914–1918). Adolf Hitler and his supporters, called Nazis, made the most of these hard times. Hitler promised to make Germany a powerful nation once again. Many Germans supported him.

After Hitler was made Chancellor in 1933, there was no stopping the Nazis and their ambitions. People who opposed him were among millions of innocent people shut up in concentration camps. Hitler dreamed of uniting the areas where German-speaking people lived into one nation. In 1938, his troops marched into Austria and then, in 1939, into Czechoslovakia. The invasion of Poland in 1939 led Britain and France to declare war on Germany. World War Two had begun.

At first, German troops overran Europe. But then the allies fought back. Hitler's first defeat came when he failed to conquer Russia. In 1944, British, Free French and American troops landed in occupied Europe, defeating the Germans in Normandy. In 1945, the Russian armies coming from the east of Europe met the British and Americans coming from the west. Hitler killed himself and his army surrendered.

Anyone who disagreed with Hitler was shut away in concentration camps. Millions died.

By 1942, Hitler and his supporters controlled much of Europe and North Africa. One country after another fell to Hitler's armies. They were powerless to prevent his advance. Britain, protected by the English Channel, was still holding out against Hitler's advancing armies. ▷

Children give the salute at a Nazi rally. The Nazis promised a brighter future. Rising prices and unemployment during the 1930s persuaded many Germans to support Hitler, who became Chancellor in 1933. ▽

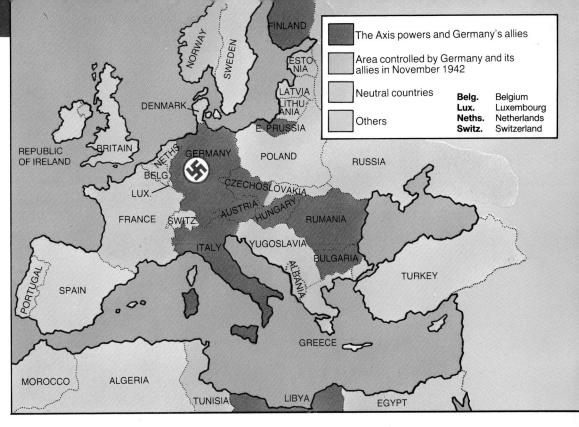

■	The Axis powers and Germany's allies
▨	Area controlled by Germany and its allies in November 1942
□	Neutral countries
▨	Others

Belg. Belgium
Lux. Luxembourg
Neths. Netherlands
Switz. Switzerland

What do you think?

Hitler's armies met with little military opposition as they marched across Europe. Crowds in some German-speaking areas of Europe greeted them with cheers. The Czech woman in this picture is giving the Nazi salute but her face shows other feelings. What do you think is making her cry?

15

Anna's sad story

'Is everything all right, Anna?' asked Mrs. Durand, cutting up some onions for their supper that night. 'Yes, Mrs. Durand,' said Anna looking down at her feet. 'Are you quite sure? You're very quiet today. Don't be afraid to ask if there's anything I can do.' 'No,' said Anna, putting on a brave face. 'I think I'll go to my room now.' 'Don't be too long. Do you want to come to the shops and meet Michèle from school later?' 'Yes, please. I'll come down soon.'

Anna soon cheered up. She enjoyed shopping with Mrs. Durand. Choosing presents to take home, and a cake for the evening meal, seemed to take her mind off whatever it was that was upsetting her. She was her old self again that evening. When the time came, Anna didn't want to go to bed. 'Let's play one more record, Michèle.' 'Okay,' yawned Michèle, 'and then I'm off to bed.'

Michèle was soon asleep, but not for long. She was woken up by the sound of Anna sobbing into her pillow. 'What's the matter, Anna?' 'Nothing Michèle. Don't worry.' 'Shall I ask Mum to speak to you?' 'No. Don't do that. I . . .' 'Aren't you enjoying your stay with us?' 'Please don't think that, Michèle. You've all been so kind. I really enjoyed our visit to Bayeux and our outing with Gran Bou . . .' Anna burst into tears again. 'Has Gran upset you, Anna?'

Drying her tears with Michèle's handkerchief, Anna protested. 'Please don't think that! You're so lucky to have your grandparents. I never see mine.' 'Oh Anna, how awful. Why don't you see them?' 'It's very muddling,'

replied Anna. 'My father's parents live in East Germany. We live in West Germany.' Michèle looked puzzled. She had not realized that there were two Germanies. 'Until the war there was only one Germany.' 'And after?' asked Michèle.

'Germany was occupied by soldiers. British, French and Americans in the West. Russians in the East. They had very different ideas about how their areas should be run,' said Anna, sitting up in bed. 'Later these occupied areas became the two new Germanies. During the war many families were split up. My father ended up in the West not knowing whether his family in the East was still alive. It was some time before he discovered that they were safe and well.'

'Surely you can visit them in the East,' asked Michèle. 'It's not that easy. You need special permission to travel in East Germany or to leave the country. My father was born in East Germany. He thinks that if he visits his family he might not be allowed to return.' 'Can you write to your grandparents in the East?' 'We can now, but I'd still rather see them.' 'Perhaps one day you will. Until then, you can share my Gran.'

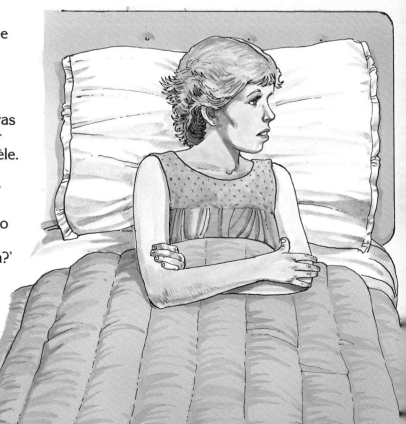

After the war, Berlin was controlled by the four allies who defeated Germany. But the three Western allies disagreed with Russia. In 1948 Russia blockaded the French, British and American parts of Berlin. The people in those parts were kept alive by a massive airlift of supplies from the West.

EVIDENCE

A view of Prague, Czechoslovakia in Eastern Europe looking much like any city in Western Europe. It is not easy to travel between the two different parts of Europe. Families are often split up and do not see each other for years.

A divided Europe

America and Russia worked together to defeat Hitler. But they did not really trust one another. By 1945, the Russian army occupied most of Eastern Europe. America feared that it might try to make further gains in Europe. The Russians were frightened that Germany might start another war, or America might become too powerful.

At the end of the war, Germany was divided into four areas. Each area was controlled by one of the four allies. Berlin itself, although it was in the Russian area, was divided between Russia, Britain, France and America. Soon there were arguments between Russia and the three Western allies. Things were so bad by 1948 that Stalin, the Russian leader, cut all road and rail links between Berlin and the areas of Germany under Western control. After 11 months of flying huge amounts of supplies into the three Western areas of Berlin, the Western countries broke the blockade.

After the blockade, Germany was divided into two parts, East and West. So was Berlin, which found itself within East Germany. Europe was split into two parts, neither trusting the other. But, in Western Europe, there was a new spirit of friendship.

This map shows the boundaries of Europe after 1948. Russia and America got on so badly after World War Two that it was said that a 'Cold War' was going on between them. This 'Cold War' divided Europe into two rival groups. The countries of Eastern Europe looked towards Russia; the countries of Western Europe towards America. The frontier between the two groups came to be known as the 'Iron Curtain'. It stretched for hundreds of miles.

A West Berlin border guard looks across from his watch tower by the Wall, into East Berlin. The Wall was built on 13 August, 1961, by the East German government. It turned West Berlin into an 'island', encircled by 165 kilometres of concrete.

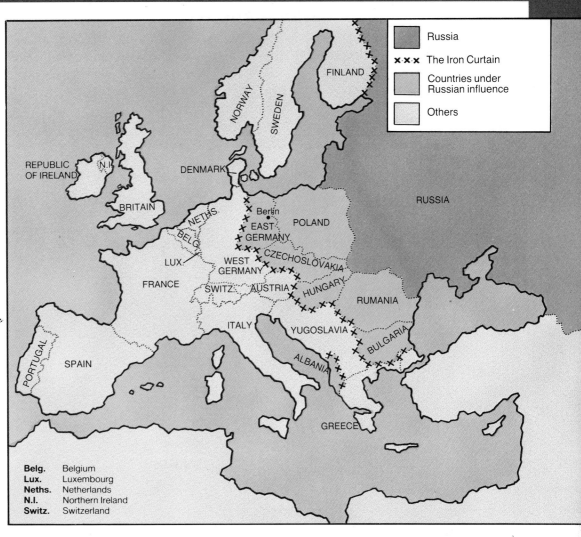

Legend:
- Russia
- ×·×·× The Iron Curtain
- Countries under Russian influence
- Others

Belg.	Belgium
Lux.	Luxembourg
Neths.	Netherlands
N.I.	Northern Ireland
Switz.	Switzerland

What do you think?

At Fulton, Missouri in America in 1946, Winston Churchill — Britain's great wartime Prime Minister — spoke of an 'iron curtain' having descended across Europe. He was not thinking of the barbed wire fences, like the one you can see in the picture on the opposite page. They did not appear until ten years after Churchill's speech. What do you think Churchill meant by an 'iron curtain'?

Six months later, Churchill called for the setting up of a kind of United States of Europe. He believed that this was the only way in which the people of Europe could enjoy a happy and peaceful future. Do you think that his idea of a United States of Europe will come true?

19

A family outing

'Michèle. Have a look at the map. Can you find where we're going?' asked Mr. Durand, looking in his rear view mirror at the three heads bouncing about in the back of the car. 'Mum, what's the name of the place we're going to?' asked Michèle. 'To an area called the Switzerland of Normandy,' answered Mrs. Durand. 'Why is it called that?' Philippe asked. 'Because the countryside is like it is in Switzerland. Hilly and rocky. But you'll see for yourself before long.' Mr. Durand drove on a bit further before Anna called out, 'I've found where we're going. Look here it is, Philippe.' Philippe had a quick look, but he wasn't very interested. He was itching to get out of the car and run about.

Philippe's chance soon came. Mr. Durand stopped the car. 'Right, out you all get and stretch your legs.' Philippe immediately ran off towards a mound of rubble and started to climb it. 'Ugh! It's so ugly here. It looks like a bomb's hit it,' said Michèle, screwing up her face. 'It's not nice to look at, but it's quite interesting,' said Mr. Durand. 'These are the remains of the St. Rémy iron works. The first job I ever had was here.' Michèle couldn't believe it. 'But there's hardly anything left. How could you have worked here?'

'It was very different when I was here,' Mr. Durand replied. 'It seemed a very busy place, full of people.' 'What happened? Where's everyone gone?' said Michèle. 'The factory was closed down and people had to move away to find work. It's sad, but it must have been very expensive to keep a small place like this open. It lost a lot of money every year.

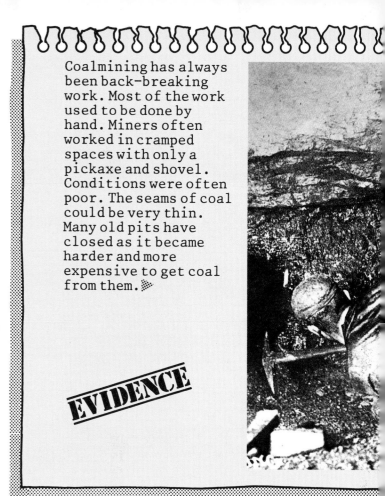

Coalmining has always been back-breaking work. Most of the work used to be done by hand. Miners often worked in cramped spaces with only a pickaxe and shovel. Conditions were often poor. The seams of coal could be very thin. Many old pits have closed as it became harder and more expensive to get coal from them.

EVIDENCE

The future of important industries is in large modern plants,' explained Mr. Durand.

'Like the ones near my home in the Ruhr Valley in Germany?' said Anna. 'I'll be seeing them on my way home tomorrow.' 'Oh, Anna. Let's not talk about tomorrow,' Michèle said quickly. Mr. Durand continued, 'Or like the big industries in the north-east of France, Anna. In the past those two areas were great rivals. It's only since the war that France and Germany have joined forces with other producers of coal and steel. We work together now to supply Europe's needs.'

Philippe came racing over to where the others were standing, his trousers covered in red dirt. 'Mum, I'm hungry.' 'All right. We'd better carry on.' They all clambered back into the car, and off they went. 'Hold tight in the back,' Mr. Durand warned. 'This is a steep hill.' They drove on for a while until Mrs. Durand spotted a good place for a picnic. 'Let's stop here,' she said. 'Just by that rock would be fine. You can stand on it and get a good view of the river in the bottom of the valley.'

Coal cutters like this one have led to great changes in the mining industry. After the war, countries in Europe worked together to produce more coal.

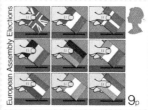

These postage stamps remind us of some important events in the Community's history:
1. Greece's entry into the Community in 1981;
2. The anniversary of the European Coal and Steel Community;
3. European elections.

Michèle's stamp album

'Michèle, Michèle, are you coming down?' 'Yes Mum, I'll be there in a minute.' 'But you said that half an hour ago. There's a letter from Germany.' There was no need for Mrs. Durand to call Michèle again. She was downstairs in seconds and was soon struggling to open the small packet. 'Be careful not to damage those stamps.' 'It's all right. I've managed. Oh, there are three envelopes inside. Two for me, and one for you.'

'How thoughtful,' said Mrs. Durand, skimming through the pages of her letter. 'Anna's parents thank us all for looking after Anna. What does Anna say?' 'It's a lovely letter, Mum.' Michèle glowed. 'She says she really enjoyed her stay with us. Listen to this bit, "Thank you for making me so welcome. You made me feel like one of the family".' 'Well, she fitted in so easily. I bet you miss her!' 'Yes I do,' Michèle agreed. 'And I'm so looking forward to seeing her again.' 'It won't be long now, Michèle. In a few weeks you'll be off to Germany. What's in the other envelope?'

'Stamps! Anna promised to send some for my album,' said Michèle, sorting them out. 'You used to collect stamps, didn't you, Mum?' 'Yes, but I never had any as colourful as these. Look at this one. It was issued to mark the 25th birthday of the European Coal and Steel Community.' 'What's that?' asked Michèle. 'Do you remember Dad telling us about the changes that have taken place in the mining and steel industries?' Mrs. Durand went on. 'He said something about working with other countries in Europe . . .'

This atomic energy plant was built, and is run by, the European Atomic Energy Community (Euratom). Euratom started its work in 1958, the same year as the Community came into operation. Its members share information on nuclear power and join together to carry out research.

EVIDENCE

'Yes,' Michèle nodded, 'he said we worked together to make the coal and steel industries stronger.' 'Exactly! Working together has helped the countries of Europe to live together in peace. Old enemies, like France and Germany, are now friends.' 'Look, Mum. Here's a stamp which marks a friendship treaty between France and Germany. I'm sure I've got one of those already.'

Michèle leafed through her album until she found a similar stamp. She was about to mount the new stamp alongside when her mother interrupted. 'You can't put that one there, Michèle. It's German, and that page is for French stamps.' 'But both stamps were issued to mark the same occasion. I'd like them to be side by side.' 'That's a nice idea,' Mrs. Durand agreed, and then went on. 'It would be better to mount them on a separate sheet. We could fill it up with other stamps which show how European countries are working together. See what you can find.'

'Will these do? They're from Italy and Belgium and mark the setting up of something called Euratom. What's that?' asked Michèle, looking puzzled. 'It's a group of European countries who work together to learn more about nuclear power,' Mrs. Durand explained. 'And here are some for the elections to the European Parliament. What heading can I put on the page?' asked Michèle. 'What about "A new community"?'

23

The Community

After World War Two, the countries of Western Europe needed to work together to rebuild their ruined farms and industries. In 1948, they formed the Organization for European Economic Cooperation (OEEC), to share out money given to them by the Americans. In 1949, the Council of Europe was set up to discuss other urgent problems.

In 1950, Frenchmen Jean Monnet and Robert Schuman put forward a scheme to help European countries to work more closely together. They suggested that the countries of Europe should allow their coal and steel industries to be controlled by one group of people. The European Coal and Steel Community (ECSC) was set up in 1951. France, West Germany, Belgium, the Netherlands, Luxembourg and Italy were the six founding members. The ECSC was very successful.

The six countries that belonged to the ECSC then made plans to work together in many other ways. This led to the European Economic Community (EEC) which started its work in 1958. The Belgian, Paul-Henri Spaak, who helped to start up the EEC, hoped that one day Europe would be united under one government.

The European Economic Community (EEC) was born with the signing of the Treaty of Rome in 1957.

THE GROWTH OF THE COMMUNITY

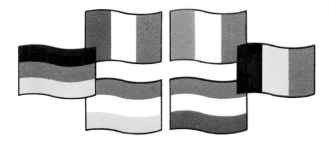

**1958**	**EEC**	West Germany, France, Italy, Belgium, Luxembourg and the Netherlands formed the EEC.
1971		Norway applied to join the EEC. In 1972, the Norwegian people voted not to join.
**1973**		After several attempts to join, Great Britain, Denmark and Ireland finally became members of the EEC.
1981		Greece became a member of the EEC.
**1986**		Spain and Portugal joined the EEC. In 18 years, the number of countries belonging to the EEC doubled, from 6 to 12.

From the Six to the Twelve. With over 320 million people, the Community has an area of about two million square kilometres. It is one of the world's richest and most densely-populated areas.

PRIVATE EYE

No. 141. Friday 12 May 67   1/6

COMMON MARKET

THE GREAT DEBATE BEGINS

Britain did not join the Community until 1973. Many British politicians were against entry. Others were sure that Britain should join. In 1961 and 1967, Britain had tried to become a member of the Community. The government of the day decided to put the arguments for and against membership to the British people. 'The Great Debate' reached the front pages of the newspapers.

'Private Eye' magazine had its own views about how far the British public was interested in the various arguments. If you could talk to one of the people in the deck chairs, what do you think they might say about the Community? What might they say now?

At the market

Michèle and Philippe stood in the middle of the market, and looked around them. 'I don't think Grandpa's coming after all, Philippe.' 'But, Michèle, he phoned to say he'd meet us here.' 'Perhaps he's changed his mind. You know he said he wouldn't visit us again after that row with Dad.' 'Perhaps he's stuck in the traffic,' Philippe said gloomily. Suddenly, Michèle pointed. 'I think I can see him.' 'Where?' 'Over there. By the flower stall.' 'Yes, that's Grandpa. Let's go and surprise him!'

Grandpa Durand laughed and joked as he led them round the market. But his mood soon changed. He was looking closely at the things on the stall. 'Are you looking for insects in the vegetables, Grandpa?' asked Michèle. Philippe giggled. 'No. I'm looking for something much more serious than that,' he replied, and carried on his close inspection.

'Are these French apples?' Grandpa demanded to know of the stall holder. 'Of course they are. I sell nothing but local produce on my stall.' 'If only there were more like you, French farmers wouldn't be in such a mess. On some of these other stalls they are selling vegetables from other countries. What good does that do French farmers?' 'Oh dear! Grandpa is getting into one of his moods,' whispered Michèle to Philippe.

They walked up to a butcher's counter. It was well stocked but Grandpa could not see what he wanted. 'Do you have any lamb?'

A march for jobs in London in 1981. The number of people out of work in Europe is growing. Some of the jobless blame the policies of their own governments, and the Community. The Community encourages a move towards fewer, bigger industrial plants. Its policy of free trade between countries leads to greater competition. Some people argue that both these things lead to fewer jobs.

EVIDENCE

As President of France, Charles de Gaulle dreamed of a Europe united under French leadership. But he did not include Britain. Here he is making a speech, in 1967, against British entry into the Community.

Pommes de Terre
Nederlandaise
5 frs.

'Certainly. Here's a fine piece of English lamb,' replied the butcher. Grandpa's face reddened. 'And what is wrong with French meat?' The butcher shrugged his shoulders and before he could answer, Grandpa was bellowing at him. 'If I buy British meat, I'm putting French farmers out of work. And why should I help the British? They're not too proud to ask for more and more from the European Community. And we're paying for it. Let them ask the Americans for help. They seem to do everything the Americans want. English lamb? Ugh! You can keep it!' With that, Grandpa stormed off. Philippe and Michèle followed at a safe distance.

On the farm

'Collecting eggs is so much easier now,' said Jacques to Michèle as they went into the hen house. 'At one time all the hens roamed around the yard. Ask your father if he can remember being sent into the orchard to find eggs. Some of the hens never seemed to lay in their nest boxes. With a deep litter house, like this one, that's one job we don't have to do.'

Michèle and Jean Pierre were spending a few days on the family farm at Caumont-sur-Orne. They always enjoyed staying with Grandpa Durand and their uncle. There were so many things to do on the farm. There were many small farms in the area. The Durand farm was typical. They had only 20 hectares of land, and, as Jacques always told his visitors, the soil was very poor.

When they had collected the eggs, Michèle and Jacques sat down on the steps of the hen house. They looked across the yard towards the orchard. 'In the old days the cattle used to graze in the orchard,' Jacques explained to Michèle. 'Mind you, I don't suppose we had more than half a dozen cows and two or three calves then. We have 50 milking cows now, and they all have to be fed. Of course we couldn't manage to grow enough food for them without a tractor and up-to-date methods. In my Grandfather's time, all the work was done with one horse – and a lot of hard work.'

Jacques was proud of the changes he had made to the farm. The cowsheds and the battery house for a thousand hens had been built since he took over.

None of the work could have been paid for without grants and loans of money from the government. But Jacques was still not satisfied.

'We work harder and get more from the land but we're just not paid enough for our eggs and milk,' Jacques complained. 'It's different for the big farmers. They're doing well all over the Community. If things don't improve for small farmers, there soon won't be any of us left.' Michèle was getting restless. There was no stopping Jacques when he started talking like this. She jumped up. 'I'd better take these eggs indoors,' she said, and ran across the yard to the farmhouse.

The Community's agricultural policy is harsh on farmers who run small farms without modern machinery. Small farms, like this one, are disappearing rapidly.

EVIDENCE

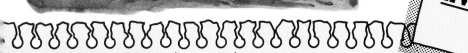

Ploughing. There are still farmers in the Community who do not have any tractors. They plough their land using oxen. There is great pressure to change, but many small farmers find it too expensive to buy new machinery.

Modern machinery is used to lift a crop of sugar beet. New crops and new methods have helped farmers to grow more food. But it has led to a drop in the number of farmworkers.

At the café

'We're back!' shouted the children as they scrambled out of Jacques's battered car. Michèle and Jean Pierre rushed out to meet their Dad. The car door slammed shut and Jacques followed, looking a bit strained. Mr. Durand greeted his brother warmly. 'Thanks for bringing the children back safely, Jacques. I hope they behaved themselves.' Jacques looked down his nose at Michèle and Jean Pierre. 'No. They were terrible,' he snapped. 'That's not fair, Uncle . . .' muttered Michèle. 'You had better go in and help your Mum,' said Dad, winking at his brother and pretending to be cross. 'How about a quick drink in the café, Jacques? It's ages since we've had a good chat.' That was just what Jacques was hoping his brother would say. 'Good idea. Work can wait a bit longer.'

In the café, Mr. Durand sipped his drink and smiled at his brother. 'It's good to remember the old days, Jacques. 'Yes,' Jacques sighed. 'Things were much better then.' Mr. Durand looked at his brother in disbelief. 'Surely you don't believe that. We're all far better off than we used to be!' 'Perhaps people that work in industry, like you, are better off,' Jacques said, frowning. 'We farmers would tell another story.' 'Farmers are always complaining!' retorted Mr. Durand. 'And with good reason,' Jacques said crossly. 'We were told the other day to cut our milk production. And it's all because of the rules made by the Community. Being a member of the Community does us no good at all.'

Mr. Durand called the waiter and ordered another two cups of coffee. He thought hard for a while.

Then he tried to explain that the Community protects farmers by making sure that they get a good price for their produce. 'Also,' Mr. Durand continued, 'we can now sell our goods throughout the Community – not just in France – without facing extra charges. That means that far more people can buy our goods.' 'But it still seems silly to me that we are not allowed to produce as much as we can,' Jacques argued. 'If we do produce more than our quota, the extra milk is sometimes thrown away. Where's the sense in that?'

Mr. Durand put some sugar into his coffee. 'It's not perfect, I know. But the Community works well for me. My small company has been selling engine parts to Germany. That could never have happened in the old days.' Jacques stirred his coffee a bit too hard. It spilled into the saucer. 'I can see we'll never agree,' he grumbled. 'Let's talk about something else. Did you watch the football last night . . . ?'

The 1984 Paris Car Show. Since the Community was formed, trade between Community countries — especially in cars — has grown rapidly.

The graph shows the rise in the number of luxury goods in French homes. Today, all Community countries are growing more wealthy. ▼

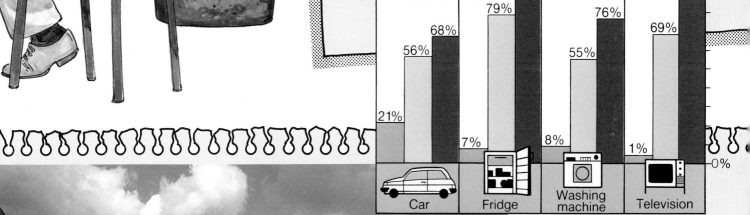

	1954	1970	1979
Car	21%	56%	68%
Fridge	7%	79%	93%
Washing machine	8%	55%	76%
Television	1%	69%	88%

EVIDENCE

◄ Britain and France worked together to produce the 'Concorde' — the world's first supersonic aeroplane. They might work together on another joint project to build a tunnel under the Channel. Do you think it's a good idea?

Trouble in the street

The house was quiet at last, or so Mrs. Durand thought as she prepared lunch. Peace was always short-lived with Michèle and Philippe around. 'Mum, Mum!' shouted the children as they charged into the kitchen. 'You'll never guess what we've seen,' said Michèle, fighting for breath. 'Lots of people shouting and waving things and . . .' said Philippe, excitedly. 'Shut up, Philippe! I want to tell Mum.' 'You shut up, Michèle. Why can't I tell Mum what we saw?' Mrs. Durand laughed. 'Calm down, you two! What's all the excitement about? Sit down and tell me all you've seen. You start, Michèle.'

Travelling abroad has made people more aware of the great variety of foods. People are more willing to try new things. Membership of the Community means that our supermarkets are full of delicious food from other Community countries.

EVIDENCE

Part of a record crop of peaches is destroyed. In some years farmers produce too much. The Community tries to ensure the farmers don't lose money. They buy up the extra and store it, or destroy it if it's likely to go bad.

'When we were walking down the road from school,' Michèle explained, 'we could hear the sound of car horns. All the traffic had stopped. There were people everywhere. And I could see a big lorry in the middle of the crowd. Someone must have parked it there on purpose to block the road.'

'When we got closer, we could see what all the fuss was about. The back of the lorry was open and crates were being thrown out onto the street.' 'Mum, they were full of eggs!' interrupted Philippe. 'What happened then, Philippe? You carry on,' said Mrs. Durand. 'As the eggs rolled out and smashed, the crowd cheered.' Philippe hesitated, and then blurted out, 'Grandpa was there! He was cheering too!' Mrs. Durand laughed. 'You really have had an adventure!'

Michèle and Philippe spoke of little else that evening. Next day the newspapers were full of accounts of what had happened. 'Just listen to this, Philippe. "Farmers forced open a lorry containing a large number of crates of British eggs. They smashed thousands of eggs in protest against government plans to cut egg production. Yet, eggs are still coming into the country from other countries within the Community."' 'Just think, Michèle. We were there.'

COMMENT

A helping hand

Throughout the world, countries used to charge other countries for all the goods that they brought into that country to sell. Most countries still do this. These extra charges, called import duties, make imported goods expensive. But the Community got rid of these duties so that now members of the Community can trade freely with each other. Many people say that this has helped to bring a better standard of living to all the people of the Community.

The Community tries to help its members in many other ways. It has agreed a fisheries policy, for instance. This aims to make sure that there are plenty of fish left in Community waters, and to protect the jobs of its fishermen. The Community also has an agricultural policy, to prevent food shortages; and it has a policy to help industry by giving money for research projects, for example.

The Community has a Regional Fund to help the poorer areas of the Community. A Social Fund gives money to help training and employment projects. The Community also helps people in other parts of the world whose lives have been ruined by famine or other disasters. Many people think it is not doing enough to help.

A tornado has destroyed their vines, but all is not lost: the Community will help them.

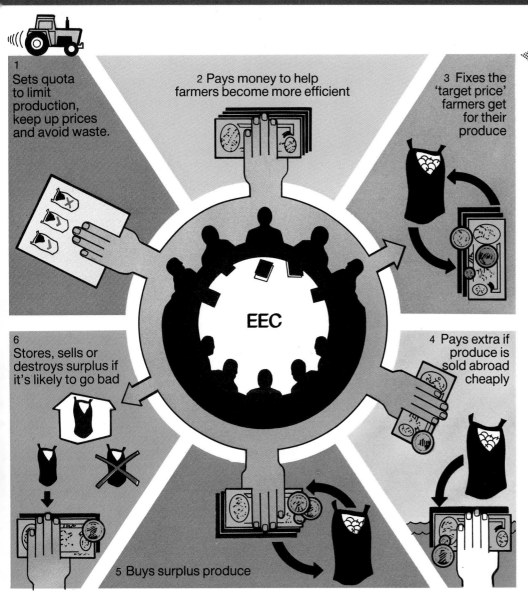

1 Sets quota to limit production, keep up prices and avoid waste.

2 Pays money to help farmers become more efficient

3 Fixes the 'target price' farmers get for their produce

EEC

6 Stores, sells or destroys surplus if it's likely to go bad

4 Pays extra if produce is sold abroad cheaply

5 Buys surplus produce

The drawing shows how the Common Agricultural Policy (CAP) works. It is called 'Common' because every member country within the Community has to obey its rules. By means of the CAP, the Community aims to:

- give farmers a fair standard of living.

- provide food at reasonable prices.

- keep farm and shop prices as steady as possible.

- make farming more efficient.

- produce enough food to meet our needs.

To protect EEC farmers, people outside the EEC face an extra charge to import food into the Community.

 What do you think?

Gateshead is a town beside the River Tyne in the north-east of England. It is one of the stations on the Tyneside Metro. The Tyneside towns received money from the Community's Regional Fund to build the Metro. There are great differences in wealth between one region and another within the Community. The Regional Fund was set up to help regions and groups with money problems. Do you think it is a good idea?

In the classroom

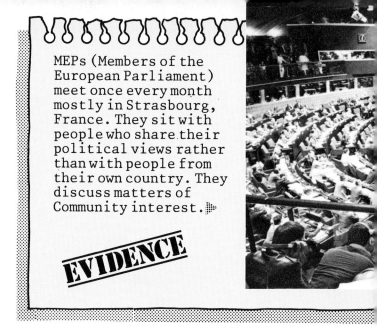

MEPs (Members of the European Parliament) meet once every month mostly in Strasbourg, France. They sit with people who share their political views rather than with people from their own country. They discuss matters of Community interest. ▶

EVIDENCE

Michèle folded her piece of paper in four and dropped it into the box at the front of the class. 'Is there anyone who hasn't voted?' asked the teacher, Mrs. Fournier. Michèle's friend, François, put her hand up. 'May I count the votes?' 'In a moment, François,' said Mrs. Fournier, sitting on the corner of her desk. 'Perhaps before we do that, you can answer a question for me. You shouldn't find it too difficult. Our class election has been held to choose the most popular figure in French history. Your parents take part in elections. Who is chosen by their votes?'

'That's easy. The President,' François answered quickly. 'Yes, that's right, François. And they also elect our local councillors and the members of the National Assembly as well. It's the National Assembly that helps to make our laws. It's like the British Parliament.'

'Our parents elect members to the European Community, don't they, Mrs. Fournier?' asked Michèle. 'I think you mean to the European Parliament, Michèle.' 'What is the European Parliament?' asked François. 'It's like a meeting to which the member countries of the European Community send representatives.' Mrs. Fournier explained. 'We send 81 representatives. There are 518 in all. They meet mostly in Strasbourg in south-east France. They discuss all aspects of Community life and they take part in small meetings, or committees, which deal with things like transport and energy. They even talk about whether teachers should be allowed to cane their pupils!'

An American Pershing missile launcher on European soil. At the moment, the European Parliament can discuss defence but does not make decisions about the defence of Europe as a whole. Do you think it should be able to do so? ⚐

'Does the European Parliament make laws like our National Assembly in Paris?' François enquired. 'Not at the moment,' replied Mrs. Fournier. 'Community laws are made by the Council of Ministers, made up of ministers from each of the member countries. They usually listen to the advice of the European Parliament. The Community has its own civil service, the Commission, to run its affairs. It's based in Brussels in Belgium. It also has its own court to settle treaty disputes between member states. But we must get back to our own election. It's almost break-time. François, you had better find out who won.' François emptied the box and counted the votes. Then the teacher announced the result: 'Pasteur 6, Napoleon 10, but Joan of Arc, 15 votes.' Michèle cheered. Her favourite had won.

The return visit

Mrs. Durand walked into Michèle's bedroom to see her throwing her clothes into a suitcase. 'What are you doing? You'll never get everything into your suitcase unless you fold your clothes properly first.' 'But it's so boring, Mum.' 'You don't want your clothes to be all creased when you get to Germany, do you?' Mrs. Durand said sternly. 'No, I suppose not, Mum.' 'Okay. Then watch how I do it.'

When the suitcase was packed, Mrs. Durand sat down on the edge of the bed. 'I think you'll like Mrs. Rockwitz. She seems to be really nice from the cards and letters we've had. Are you looking forward to seeing Anna again?' 'I can't wait for tomorrow,' Michèle said excitedly.

'I think we'd better check you've got everything you need,' said Mrs. Durand, wrinkling up her forehead. 'I'll make a list to make sure you don't leave anything behind. Perhaps we ought to check them together. I'd put your identity card in the front pocket of your shoulder bag where you can get at it easily.'

'I was hoping I'd have to get a passport,' sighed Michèle. 'You'll have one soon,' replied Mrs. Durand. 'But you won't need one to travel in Germany or any other country within the Community. They accept the identity cards which we all have to carry at home. As you're only ten . . .' 'Nearly eleven, Mum.' '. . . nearly eleven, you'll need to take this form which Dad and I have signed. It gives you our permission to travel out of the country. We had to get it from the mayor's office.'

'Mum, I read somewhere that you should take out medical insurance before travelling abroad.' 'I hope you're not going to be ill!' said Mrs. Durand in dismay. 'Not if I can help it.' 'I should think not. The school has made some arrangements to cover sickness or accidents and, in any case, you can make use of the German hospitals and doctors. Anna could have used our health services when she was here. It's been possible to do that within the European Community for some time now.'

'Take care of your German currency,' Mrs. Durand warned. 'Remember, the German mark is worth about three French francs.' 'Can I spend francs in Germany since we're both members of the Community?' Michèle asked. 'One day we might have the same money. We might have Eurodollars instead of francs or marks. Not everyone wants that. We share many things in the Community, but we enjoy our differences.' Mrs. Durand put the German currency into Michèle's purse, and tucked it into a pocket of her shoulder bag. 'I think that's it. All you need now is sleep, Michèle.' 'I'm too excited to sleep!' 'Well, you'll just have to try. Goodnight.' 'Goodnight, Mum.'

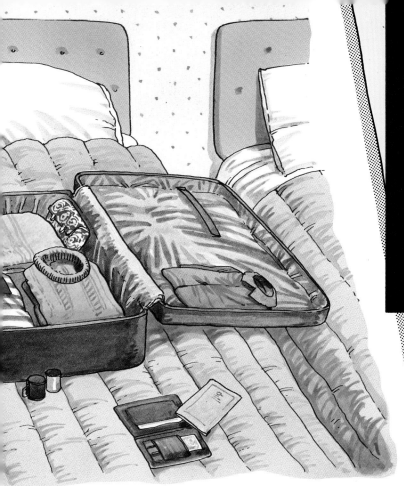

These are the 11 currencies of the 12 Community countries. Belgium and Luxembourg have a common currency. Will they all use Eurodollars one day?

EVIDENCE

The boundaries between countries in the Community are still marked by customs posts. But now it is much easier to travel between the countries. ▼

The future

In a short time, the Community has achieved many things. The Community was set up to boost the economies of the member countries. It still aims to encourage trade. But it also has policies as varied as equal opportunities for men and women, and caring for the places where we live and work.

There are still many problems to be sorted out and the Community has plenty of critics. It's expecting a lot of member countries always to put the Community's interests before their own. Another problem is that the richer countries within the Community worry that their progress is being slowed down by the poorer countries. And with more countries hoping to join, the Community might become too big and clumsy. These difficulties will not go away overnight. But at least now they can be talked about in a friendly way, and not fought over on the battlefield.

Perhaps one day there will be a United States of Europe with one government, one language, one currency. But today, not everyone wants a closer union. Although member countries accept laws and policies made by the Community for the Community, they are proud of their independence.

Greek farmers at work. The EEC might split in two: rural south against the industrial north.

These Basque terrorists are not interested in a large, united Europe. They want a small, independent Basque country in which they can have a greater say in how their lives are governed. They use violent bombing campaigns to try and achieve what they want. In 1985, on the day that Spain and Portugal signed the Treaty of Rome, Basque terrorists killed several people as a protest.

The Basque terrorists are a violent group. But in some ways they express the fears of many people in Europe who would prefer to belong to smaller units, enjoying greater variety. These people want their laws to be made by people from their own country, and not by the European Parliament which might not understand, or care about, local problems. Do you think a united Europe is a good thing?

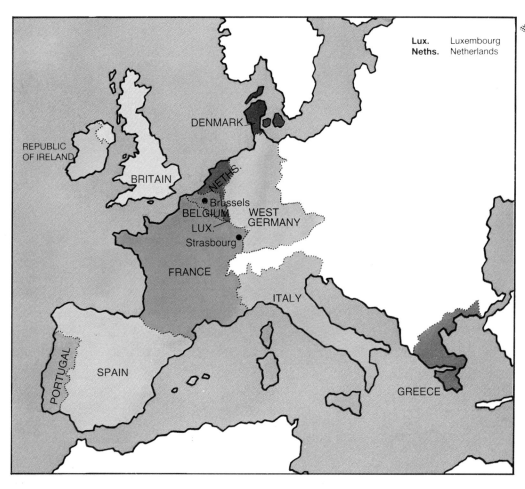

Lux. Luxembourg
Neths. Netherlands

DENMARK

REPUBLIC OF IRELAND

BRITAIN

NETHS.

• Brussels
BELGIUM
LUX.
Strasbourg

WEST GERMANY

FRANCE

ITALY

PORTUGAL

SPAIN

GREECE

This map shows the 12 countries of the Community. The area is densely peopled. It is well-provided with raw materials, so industry accounts for most of its wealth. Farming is also of great importance. A good transport system between the countries enables people and goods to be easily moved. Do you think that any other countries may want to join the Community? Why do you think that some countries in Western Europe are not interested in belonging to the Community?

41

Find out more

The horrors of two world wars encouraged the nations of Western Europe to forget their differences. Since 1945, they have learnt to work together. The European Economic Community came into operation in 1958 to bring about even closer cooperation. People and goods can now move about the Community with greater ease than ever before.

The setting up of the European Community was the first step towards uniting the countries of Western Europe. The Community is concerned with many of the things we do, from the price of the food we eat, to the weight of the lorries that drive on our roads.

Members of the Community do not always agree with one another. But they share the common aim of bringing about a new community in Europe. Not everyone who lives within the Community thinks this is a good idea. What do you think?

In 1981 the Organisation of African Unity (OAU) met in Nairobi, Kenya. Leaders from all OAU countries meet once every year to discuss problems and settle disputes. The Community has trade agreements with the OAU. ▷

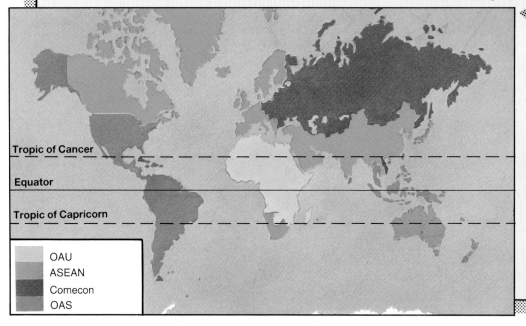

Tropic of Cancer

Equator

Tropic of Capricorn

OAU
ASEAN
Comecon
OAS

◀Other countries in different parts of the world sometimes meet together because they have similar interests. This map shows four of these groupings: the Organization of American States (OAS), Comecon, the Organization of African Unity (OAU), and the Association of South East Asian Nations (ASEAN).

In 1983 this gas pipeline was laid by engineers working for the Council for Mutual Economic Assistance (Comecon). It carries gas from the gasfields in Russia to some Communist countries in Eastern Europe. Comecon members, which include Cuba and Vietnam, work together to improve their economies. ▼

Things to do
Collect Stamps
Build up a collection of stamps telling the story of the Community.

Contact an MEP
Try to find out the name of your MEP. You could write and ask them about their work.

Twin Towns
Does your town have a twin in the Community? Find out about your twin town. Does your school run an exchange scheme? Contact International Pen Friend, Box 340, Dublin 12, Ireland to find a pen friend in the Community.

Books to read
Most of the books written about the European Community are for older readers. But they have good pictures. Here are some your teacher might help you to get.
Focus on the EEC, M.W. Thomas, Nelson, 1973.
Western Europe after Hitler, B.J. Elliot, Longman, 1968.
Europe 1763–1970, Hugh Gough, Longman, 1976.
Write to the Commission of the European Communities, 8 Storey's Gate, London SW1P 3AT for information on the Community.

Time chart

1945 World War Two ended in Europe.

1946 Churchill's 'United States of Europe' speech.

1949 Council of Europe set up by 10 West European countries to discuss matters of common interest.

1948 Berlin blockaded. The 'Cold War' began. Organization for European Economic Cooperation (OEEC) set up.

1951 Treaty of Paris signed by France, Italy, West Germany, Belgium, Luxembourg and the Netherlands, set up the European Coal and Steel Community (ECSC).

1957 Treaty of Rome signed by the 'Six' – the original members of the Community: France, Italy, West Germany, the Netherlands, Belgium and Luxembourg. It set up the EEC and Euratom.

1958 The EEC and Euratom started to work. Planning began on the Common Agricultural Policy.

1961 Britain, Ireland, Denmark and Norway applied to join the EEC.

1963 De Gaulle prevented Britain's entry to the EEC.

1967 Britain, Ireland, Denmark and Norway re-applied for membership.

Britain's entry blocked by de Gaulle again.

1969 Leaders of EEC countries agreed to enlarge the Community.

1970 Talks held between leaders of EEC countries about the proposed entry of Britain, Ireland, Denmark and Norway into the Community.

1971 EEC agreed that the above countries could join. British House of Commons accepted British entry into the EEC by 356 votes for, to 244 against.

1972 Norwegian people voted in a referendum not to join the EEC.

1973 Treaty of Brussels. Britain, Denmark and Ireland become members of the EEC.

1975 A referendum was held in which British people voted 2–1 to stay in the EEC.

1979 First elections to the European Parliament.

1981 Greece joined the EEC.

1983 Common Fisheries Policy agreed.

1985 Spain and Portugal signed the Treaty of Rome.

1986 Spain and Portugal officially become members of the EEC.

Keywords

CAP Common Agricultural Policy. Laws to do with farming that all member countries should obey.

Cold War A time of tension between America and Russia after World War Two.

Commission Deals with the day-to-day running of the Community's business. It is based in Brussels in Belgium.

Council of Ministers A group of politicians from each Community country who make laws for the Community.

Currency Money.

Customs Money (duties or taxes) paid when goods are moved from one country to another.

ECSC The European Coal and Steel Community. It was set up by six countries in 1951 to help their coal and steel industries.

EEC The European Economic Community. 12 European countries now belong to it. It started its work in 1958.

Euratom The European Atomic Energy Community. European countries joined together in 1958 to research into nuclear power.

European Parliament The place where Community matters are discussed by MEPs (Members of the European Parliament). It mainly meets in Strasbourg in France.

Exports Goods sold by one country to another.

Imports Goods bought by one country from another.

Industry The production of things for us to use or consume.

OEEC The Organization for European Economic Cooperation. It was set up in 1948 to help rebuild farms and industries that were destroyed in World War Two.

Quota A limit to the amount that people are allowed to produce, or have.

Surplus More than enough of an item.

Target price A fixed price for produce set by the Council of Ministers.

Unemployment When people are unable to find jobs.

Index

Illustrations appear in **bold** type

Illustrations
Peter Dennis/Linda Rogers Associates
Back cover, 4–5, 8–9, 10–11, 12, 16–17, 20–21, 22–23, 26–27, 28–29, 30, 31, 32–33, 36–37, 38–39
Raymond Turvey maps 11, 15, 19, 41, 42; diagrams 25, 31, 35

Photographs
Aldus Archive: 12, 15L, 24
J. Allan Cash Photolibrary: 29T, 39B
Barnabys Picture Library: 13, 18
B.B.C. Hulton Picture Library: 27
Camerapix Hutchison Library Ltd: 29B
John Cornwell: 20
E.E.C. Joint Research Centre, Petten: 23
French Tourist Board: coverT
Robert Harding Picture Library: 12–13, 28
Imperial War Museum: 11T, 14, 15R
Jean Guy Jules/ANA: 33
Photos Lecluse: 9B
Novosti: 43
Photo Source: 17T, 19
Popperfoto: coverB, 26–7, 34
Private Eye: 25
Rex Features Ltd: 36–7, 41
Roger-Viollet: 8, 9T, 11B
Spectrum Colour Library: 17B, 40
Frank Spooner Pictures: 31T, 42–3
Tyne & Wear Passenger Transport Executive: 35
Waitrose, a branch of the John Lewis Partnership: 32
ZEFA: 21, 31B